PERSONAL LOGISTICS

ABOUT THE AUTHOR

Chris Palazzolo was born in Perth, Western Australia in 1966. He studied literature, philosophy and communications at Murdoch University before pursuing an economically hazardous life as an Australian writer. He can turn his hand to poetry, short fiction, long fiction and non-fiction, and has been shortlisted for a handful of national awards including the ABC Fiction Award in 2009 and the Seizure Viva La Novella Award in 2014. *Personal Logistics* is his first book with Fremantle Press. He lives in the East Kimberley region of north-western Australia with his wife and three children.

PERSONAL LOGISTICS

CHRIS PALAZZOLO

FREMANTLE PRESS

For Meredith

CONTENTS

AUTHOR NOTE

The poems in this collection were written in Kununurra, Western Australia, between 2019 and 2023. My family and I had moved to Kununurra from Perth in early 2019 for my wife to take up a position as an accountant at Wunan, an Indigenous not-for-profit organisation. After we'd placed the kids in the local school, I'd found some time off from domestic chores to pursue my intellectual hobbies in the Kununurra Public Library. My first writings were mainly diary entries and letters to friends and family curious about our hasty migration (recessionary conditions in Perth in 2018). After about three months, I had settled into a writing routine and had begun to draft the first of the poems that appear here.

These drafts evolved from the diary entries. We'd arrived in the middle of the 'build-up', a diabolical three or so months of intense heat (average 42° Celsius) and extreme humidity (80%) that precedes the monsoon. In the peak heat of the day I'd go into a kind of apocalyptic trance, with out-of-body experiences and weird visions of cosmic calamities visited from the sky. I began to write the entries in a more elliptical, shorthand style, not necessarily because I was aiming to write poetry, but because the climate was forcing on me a more economical type of expression. Naturally, the climate featured very strongly in these early poems – the heat and sweat, the stink of bins and rot, and the storms of the monsoon – the pounding rains, wild winds, and lightning so vivid it makes night broad daylight.

Before long I began to acclimatise. The dry season of warm days, cool nights and low humidity began, and my poetic musings moved on to the human life and its impacts on the region – its industries, transport systems, demographics and histories. I called the final collection *Logistics* because that term seems a useful cover-all that takes into account all of these factors and their interrelationships. I made a conscious decision to not divide the collection into chapters or sections; however, readers will observe that there is design in the arrangement. Joining it all together are the twin poems called 'Tribute'. The protagonist of these poems is of course the mighty Ord River. The Ord makes possible all the human activity of this region: the Indigenous nations that have lived here for millennia; the modern town and industries dependent on the Ord irrigation and hydroelectric schemes.

Writing poetry is popularly spoken of (in Australia at least) as a kind of mystical form of personal expression. Poetry is 'pure emotion in words', it comes about because of 'a visit from the muse', certainly not from anything as vulgar as effort. The reality though is that writing poetry is a craft and, like all crafts, requires learnt skills and steady application.

I think it is useful, and not at all devaluing, to think of a poem as a machine: a tooled assemblage of moving parts that is operated by a reading. The purpose of such a machine is to give aesthetic and intellectual pleasure, and to leave a lingering impression in the mind of the reader. Like any machine, a poem is constructed. The site of its construction is a vast workshop of parts and tools called (in the anglophone world) The English Language. Some forms of poetry like sonnets and sestinas have strict rules of construction – the rules of a sonnet for instance precede any given sonnet. Other kinds of poetry like blank verse have more flexible rules; I would argue, internally generated rules. This doesn't mean that blank verse has no rules: every successful poem has some kind of 'endoskeleton', an internal structure and logic that makes it a singular, individuated utterance. I call that singularity, that individuality, its 'music', a productive consonance of the sonorousness of words and phrases, and the meanings they signify.

Some may find it instructive to know my working methods, that is to say, how I go about trying to find the music in my notebook scribblings. I like to use the term *wherewithal* as a starting point. *Wherewithal* is very important. Without *wherewithal* there is no writing at all. *Wherewithal* is tending to my own 'personal logistics': me packing my bag – after my family have gone to school and work – going to the library, setting up my pad and pens and putting pen to paper; or, staying up late, after everyone is in bed, sitting at the table and putting pen to paper there. I sit over that page, sometimes up to an hour, waiting for an opening line on any subject to present itself. When something promising pops into my mind I write. I call this the 'something from nothing' moment. Each draft consists of a page, say twenty lines, sometimes more, sometimes less. I will do this morning and night for two weeks until I have about twenty drafts. After that I will go through each draft and try to find some interesting turn of phrase, a choice of word, change of tense or shift in tone; anything that can be worked on and teased out into a poem. Redraftings can sometimes yield results quickly – I'll have a working poem within a couple of sittings – but sometimes it can take years, the drafts put aside in dusty notebooks, or transferred from USB to USB, before the right words to make it work come to me. But the outcome has to be the linguistic music of poetry: a singular and (dare I say it) organic utterance. To quote Yeats, *if it does not seem a moment's thought / Our stitching and unstitching has been naught.*

Kununurra, 2023

In all Things, all Things service do to all:
And thus a Sand is Endless, though most small.

Thomas Traherne, Christian Ethicks

TRIBUTE

Light and air surround my pen
which will now ink some phrases
            about water.

Water. Water it is
that makes the diodes emit light.
Water it is that makes the fan blades
            feather the air.
Water; skeleton-crushing tonnes of it
falling every second on turbines.

It takes a hop, skip and switch-flick –
the intercession of a thralled eye –
to convert a river into a poem,
a quantum of the arrogance
that seized its flowing
            in Paleocenic gorges.

    Hear the roar of it
            Feel the spray of it
                in every word herein!

EMPIRE OF THE INANIMATE

The wing looks so rigid
but the forces impacting on it
make it impossible to imagine
that anything as frail as a human hand
rested on its slat, maybe for balance
as the other hand lined the rivet gun
along the seam; what horror of whipping
tendon-ripping death
would flick away that human
should he miraculate there now?

That's exactly the kind of morbid
and idle thought that comes
in the comfort of compressed air
and soft seats, the vaguely apprehended
peril of a few centimetres of fuselage
separating you from the eternal
ballooning suction. The seconds
of the 24-hour flight plan
pass so sensibly you can set your watch
by the drinks trolleys; but out there
nucleated moments billow out
like lungs in too much air screaming
to purge thought; they empty of time
to merge with that gulf
of atmospheres and sunlight.

Perhaps the almost touching Death,
adjacent to your cup of in-flight coffee,
pricks your imagination with horror
should you relax to thinking
that the empire of the inanimate
can always be slipped past
at the price of a flight ticket?

LAW AND PHYSICS

To get the car I have to sign.
So easy; five quick squiggles on forms
to bind me and the machine
in a kind of circuitry of power limits;
traffic codes and capped explosións
granting me free passage on the roads.
The terse friendliness of the salesman,
his steady hand lifting the forms
for my shaky hand to sign, declares
that the birthright of all men
will be conferred on me
when those forms receive my unique
ink-marks; the constrained freedom
of internal-combustion propulsion,
the precision bleed and concentrated
firepower that opens the cosmos
like a fruit. To each man in this yard
it's as thoughtless as a tendon flex –
a wrist flick that pushes a pen
and turns an ignition key
starts another industrial revolution.

ON SEEING BEAGLE GULF

My first glimpse of a sea
since our migration didn't comfort me
with cold oblivion; it was blue
as it shouldn't be, too smooth, too gassy –
and projecting my swimming
child phantasm of a life that may never
have been was impossible.

That has always, *always* been
my flashing other being,
the anti-me that's me on the anti-shore.
He drowned. I woke.
Each one cancelled the other
and yet each one happened,
and the drowning water, black and sheer,
I'm always in it now
even as I mark the fortieth year
of the life I was hauled onto a beach to live.

Silly isn't it. That northern sea
with its wavelets obscured by steam,
looked like an abstraction, a schema
of a sea, paradoxically hard,
as if the water had frozen at 24° Celsius
to form an oblique pane
at the vanishing point of my middle age.
Maybe it was just my aging eyes

cataracted with jade, but I looked
from that foreshore and thought
of Vonnegut worms tickling the sky;
I knew I would never meet me
in that too smooth too blue sea.

TRAVEL ELLIPSES

Those farthest lines of where I'm not –
new seas I could never swim back from –
vapour trails from a quantum of humanity
too far for my instrument eyes to see.

But I have trod deep water and reclined
in soft seats in pressurised tubes,
and I've left each one of me swimming
and flying forever; even if there is less of me,
I hold my kids and kiss my wife
when a reduced me returns –
all of me, lost in the sea, the infinite
depthless skies, loves them no less than I do.

OUTSIDE NEWMAN

The condition of the men
who explored this land
can only be imagined,
but I have passed through it
painlessly, a little strung out
on caffeine perhaps,
a little traumatised
by hours of sedentary tension;
minute modulations
of muscular contractions
to swerve this way and that
but not onto a shoulder
or into a road train's axle.
The land, inconceivable
miles of it, streams past
near the shoulders,
turns steadily, slowly
farther out, while that strangely
detached spar of trees or mountains
on a waterless sea
doesn't seem to move at all.

Evening. I count the seconds
by the listless flicking
of motel tv channels.
Outside Newman, men move
around like showered phantoms

texting spouses to relieve
the arid hours –
men food piled high
in the bain-maries,
men quarters smelling
of potpourri and farts.
I feel so frail amid all this men
hardness, though hard boots
make men's feet soft in thongs,
    easily wounded.

REMOTE HIGHWAY

Driving so fast for so long
I feel afterimages of me
    slip off me
like the old cartoons
of foiled predators;
seated spirits startled
by their disembodiment,
disappearing like
steam in sunlight,
watching a car they thought
they were safe in
leave them behind
on sections of highway
only mulga, hummock
and kangaroo carcass inhabit.

I'm tired and sore.
The images must be a fright,
showing ribs
through translucent shirt
and flaps of skin,
    skull-teeth sneer –
my eyes have wandered off
      the road again!

Seek the roadhouse –
pergola shade

and black coffee magic
to rob my future vitality
for another 200ks of rolling
bitumen and bolting white lines.

A 10-YEAR STUDY
OF A SINGLE SHADE OF BLUE

I love how the mulga doesn't call –
it doesn't say come further
find more of me –
it doesn't because more is all there is.

It is wrapped off in an openness
absolute and utterly passive –
identity, agency, subjectivity are a joke
like the ridiculous biting bull-ant
and the absurd Gilbert's dragon.

Wander off the highway's shoulder
into the dimensionality of same trees –
from the monad to your senses
observe witch's brooms at every turn
and scribbles of shadows no shelter.

When the ticking of your engine
is inaudible you are lost –
that puny thread of bitumen
will never be found again.

It's not your metaphysics
in that single shade of blue –
if you're a flap of leather
in a hat, shirt and pants

don't ever say the mulga called you –
said come further
find more of me –
it didn't because more is all it ever was.

HALLS CREEK

This is the one-hand-clap town,
the one you wonder is it really here;
a hush so deep on these wild wide streets
that bloke in the mulga
        could be the last resident leaving.

You find others; eat fish and chips
and drink coke in a beer garden
with a desert beside the fence;
you make the AGM with minutes spare,
   deliver the reports before 'God's Work'.

But you never completely unwind;
the to and from is too long for that;
the here too small to really exist
and work stress absurdly
disproportionate to its size,
while always on your eardrum
the engine thrum from the shock
of kilometres that never get shorter,
for a town that never gets closer
                until you're in it.

READING *BEING AND NOTHINGNESS*
AT PARDOO ROADHOUSE

   Nothing is going to save you
from no longer being,
for there is being
only non-being,
and that is being – that's it –
always and forever (until death) –
      being is fleeing
and its residue,
watching from non-being,
an echo designated consciousness.

   Consciousness. Yes! Mourning
the missing now. It all makes sense.
That fluorescent bar makes sense,
that tv bracket makes sense,
in a donga the very essence of which
is a fraught relationship
   to Here. After all, what's
my Here, my Now,
after 1900ks of driving?
            Not landscapes,
   Not scenery – a car cabin
ponging of sweat
and spilled thermos coffee.

     I saw Port Hedland today
         for the first time in my life.
     I didn't really see it

because there was nothing to see;
    from the bypass
it is a far proximity,
  an empire
monstering so delicately
so spindly powerlined across a plain
of grasses, rail, and oxide mounds –
a white sky too big for human eyes,
some thin cloud, low, to the south.

    I missed it, in the same way
consciousness misses the Now –
and that was the truest consciousness –
the soft pupa of muscle and bone
making the machine go –
the steady pressure of the foot –
the torsion of arms and hands –
ever alert eyes
       darting on gauges,
          blinking
the dust smear of refracted light –
       a cyborg equipoise
which has its place
thinking, responding – for they're our
machines out there on that red world
extracting their own matter –
      but somewhere inside
where the metaphysical parts
of our machines reside
I knew the terror of kinship
with transformers and wharves.

OUTER SPACE

Some words on any square metre
of highway bitumen you care to think upon,
out that way, or in that direction,
past the last lights of town,
and beneath the ragged hem of stars,
a sublime and arbitrarily singled out
mat of modern human industry,
which once knew the back of a shovel
and the sole of a boot – but that's the extent
of intimacy with its fabricators – now
knows tyre tread, kangaroo and goanna foot,
the sun during his blazing hours
and night black as the ink
                    that dries on this page.

    Now, why; why the hyperfocus
on a patch of tarred bluestone –
Is it safety you seek? Or is it the infinite?
Or can only the astronaut behind
                those high beams answer that?

KUNUNURRA FOOTPATHS

Black feet, white feet;
they all resemble camel feet
on these streets – the deliberative tread,
and the pale, cushioned soles,
an ankle, not quite a fetlock,
but an articulated bolt and swivel
of bone hoisting an animal
whose thoughts up there,
closer to the sun,
shielded by centimetres
of hat brim, extend to no more
rarefied dimensions than the next step,
which is, of course, a matter
of the purest metaphysics
to the camel – I walk, I am;
for the beings of camels and men
synthesised a century before
these streets were laid, the flyblown
union of hoof and sole trudging
                    a hypostatic desert floor.

ONE VOTE ONE VALUE

For 120 years the argument went
five of them made one of us,
not because we were five times
more substantial but five times less.
Inhuman distance made us spectral
unless we filled us in with their power,
their careless decisive ballot drops;
to give the embrace of the state
a warmth even spectres can feel
suffrage was transfused like ectoplasm.

Well the good stuff has stopped now
and in our awakening we realise
we are lost beyond any meaningful
involvement in those affairs;
our forms which break sunlight
on the Kimberley dirt find fellowship
in the disappointment of seasons,
the pride of barren ridges
and the sweat we share on skins
as likely black as white; for if five
is for spectres and zero is for slaves,
            one is for human beings.

COLLECTIVE
For Charles Court

As big as the land itself –
                    Human Organisation.

He blew up a mountain back in 1965
but bringing men up here to move that half kilometre
of subsided rubble under the sun entailed energy use
of tectonic force. The road, fence and dam that engrid the land
competes with the land itself; he argues, as he digs
and burns and demolishes, you've had your turn,
for hundreds of millions of years,
but with Capital at my right and Labour at my left
to make a great flood for the new Genesis
                    I'm pre-eminent now.

Humans, scattered all over the land now,
we're as Organised as ants,
                    of One Mind as ants.

The Mind – One – under the Sun –
                    Is Organisation.

DEMONS

Wyndham: the poorest child
in the state's attic. No poky barred window
above him; a steamed-up smoke-dirt sky
so hot it's as suffocating as a low
ceiling he stuffs himself under on a bunk.
His eyes may behold infinite space; a gulf
for fishing, a floodplain for an ancient parliament;
but in landforms reduced to the most cursory contours,
they can never be deceived; the department
demons sent his aunts and uncles beyond
that plain. Go to hell and prosper, the demons said.

When the cousins returned their eyes didn't blink
and their mouths never spoke; but at night
he heard voices whisper *Oombulgurri*
                              from the top bunk.

KIMBERLEY THUMBNAIL SKETCHES

1. Geology

The amount of Earth out there
pulls on me, sends my phrases
chasing echoes of some hollow conceit.

All of it out there – the dirt, the loose stones,
the rock piled on rock – doesn't judge
or hector or engage in any way
with any of it; it doesn't see, it doesn't
hear, doesn't feel; chthonic, in-itself
ad infinitum, it has not lain for 100s
of millions of years, nor will it lay for 100s
of millions more; that is human conceit.
It is forever now, always and evermore Now.

2. Climate

I forget how big it is
when it sleeps under that bright
dry blue and cold mist stars.

But when it wakes I realise again
how small I am; that shift before all
my senses at the step of the door
is the swell of the Land rising
to its monstrous green and savage self,
a Gaian fever bursting seed, egg and womb.

For the next five months
it will be awake, its metabolism will race
at a steady 42° Celsius, its mountains
will take lightning strikes
and reptiles will rule the night.

3. History

Here nations of the mind
jostled on gestures and agreements
and songs and fights which were all
worked around
forgottenrememberedforgotten etc
because time didn't exist, only Earth.

Here nations of the mind woke to time
in a surveyor's glass – a ghost
cleaved to the Law of book and gun –
and strange animals grazing the Earth.
From chain, stock and saddle
they watched time's bills
pared like skin off the fruit of the Earth.

Time begat wages – wages begat labour –
labour begat time etc – the Earth
was engridded with road, fence and dam.
Loosed, nations in negative slide
across the Earth, losing skin on rigid edges.

4. Society (and me)

The boom boxes are the night's
racing heartbeat. It is a sleepless animal –
it stinks of rot and smokes and bat.

I try to sleep, under fans, without sheets,
but wakefulness draws me to my lawn.
I hear a nation in negative, still at war,
burn energy all hot foetid night –
the squeals of chasey kids
(who play while my kids dream)
give me the chill of the alien.

NATIONS IN NEGATIVE
On the defeat, by referendum,
of the Indigenous Voice to Parliament, 2023

My guess is they're fights
over very old slights
and all the mobs seem to know
            when to have them.

I suspect it's that old woman
who holds the calendars,
the date pencilled on a star;
when it's time to sit on a footpath
and ignore my passing 4wd.

My theory is it's a signal
for that mob to quarrel with that mob
in the carpark of Coles
a whole block away;
enmities from an aeon ago
blooded by some fresh insult
transmitted through town walls
as if they're not there.

But who am I that suspects
and guesses, I of the idle
anthropological muse?
            I am the ghost
with the shopping bags.

It's for me to presume and judge,
and discard any scruples
like dockets in the trolley,
for what's wrong
with wanting to shop in peace?

Let the teeth and blood
hosed from the dawn lockups
speak for the mashing of Indigeneity
                on brick, glass and cop.

A NATIVE TITLE CLAIM
ON A COMMUNITY NOTICE BOARD, WYNDHAM.

In the beginning was the Word
seeded in deep time
before the Magna Carta, before John,
before the first wedge in the stone of Enlil.
The Word is Law.
The Law is Title.

What an odd companion this claim,
with its tribunal number,
makes to the pinned ads for boat trailers
and netball club memberships.

There's nothing ordinary for me
in the doorway of this broiling Wyndham day
but it is just another day
for the two girls at the checkout.
I watch them pass into the white heat
with their coke and coffee chill
and I imagine they've stepped through a portal
into an Era of their own Sovereignty,
as old as geology, won for them
by their elders using these instruments
of the Common Era. It's as if I gaze out
from the air-conditioned gloom
through a fissure I have no right
to pass through for it is prised open by God
onto the thought-erasing infinity of Him.

SONGLINES AND SANDY FLOORS

The courtiers arrive in 4wds
for yarns and barbeque barra,
commiserations on a closing mine
and whistles over a gun the cops
consign to memory if not yet a database.

The boys raising dust with my daughter
beyond the drum's flamelight
bind this gathering to songlines
woven across land and sea;
ancestors' songs strung, beyond memory,
in trade, disputes and love.
Even when the big ships
brought grazing animals with the Gun
and Law still these songs were sung,
in long treks north chancing fence
and freehold, and sea voyages south
through imperial shipping lanes;
they were singing the day
a directive from Canberra, a deployment
to our protectorate in the Timor Sea,
led the Jaru soldier
            to marry the daughter of Dili.

Now they are royalty of our street
and this Australasian romance
every day runs sand through my house
            off their noisy princes' feet.

GARDENING AND SEMIOTICS

Trying to capture in language
my hands grabbing clumps of sun-stiffened,
mulch-rotted, dusty-sheafs-
of-rib-cage-showing-sepulchral-smelling leaf-litter
under dappling tree shade
would exhaust an entire lexicon so infinitely variably
alike the forms the leaves have assumed
as inanimate things in the red loam;
they are singularly impossible to remark upon
except that one which clings briefly
to my forearm; glued by sweat
and streaked dirt, the sensation
makes me think of a spider and I brush it off in a panic.

If outer space is no space at all
then infinite variableness is not the kind of difference
that words need for grip. Only as a catalyst
for human action can a dry leaf
enter the language; so here it is,
pinned in syntax – a spider defending its patch
against a blundering human – the starring predicate
in my poem of raking and weeding
to reclaim the beds from nature. Meanwhile,
above my shoulders, a hundred million green hopefuls
          rustle their hustle in a breeze.

MY GARDEN

My garden wouldn't be so dull if I dreamed it –
my eye wouldn't be so flat and my limbs
wouldn't ache so pitifully with reluctance –
for in a dream its shabby corners would be mysteries
the haze of popped seed husks and pillows of webs
a bed for a hazardous day sleep –
weeds that have long usurped the grass
are green enough for a squint pretend
and when I drop my rake I will lie
and watch the blue between the tree squiggles –
watch and drowse, until a cloud rumble a terror
                    I can never survive waking.

My garden if I dreamed it would mean love in its thickets
wisdom in its beds, peace in its leaf littered rockeries –
I would work in it every day, all day,
and even as the shadows stretch
and the haunting quality of afternoon toil troubles me
                    I would never abandon it.

'

THE CRICKET

That is a very simple machine
stripped to three basic components –
spring-latch legs to spring it away
attached to a libido like a battery
with five days of life in it
generating energy
for an enormous voice-box
which emits a mating call
so loud, so unflagging
and needling, my ears
are ringing whenever it stops.
The sound drills my eardrums
relentlessly. It drives every thought
that's not of it from my mind.
But I can never find the bugger.

How furious is the universe
in the smaller life that inhabits it –
this creature will never know quiet
never know rest or play
or ease of any sort; call call call
with all its might for a mate,
unspring the torment to an offspring.

WALKING THE DOG

The footpath is a magic piddle text
she reads with her exquisite nose –
so compelling she'll choke herself
for its conclusion, then jerk me off my feet
to squirt her own quick review.

It's hardly a secret society,
dog society; they fight and pal,
root and poo completely without guile,
and yet there are mysterious subtexts
in a dog's interaction with its peers,
instant evaluations on which spots
to decode, on what to dart hither thither
across those trails that glow
       for her nose only –
why select a urine scrawl on the driveway
but not around the lamppost?
why ignore the fence-straddling brute
but fight the whelping bitch?
is it the mark of a sundered sibling
          she seeks,
   to trigger a memory
of a squirming litter?
Her mind's choice
     spikes her to the kerb –
the quickest instinctual compulsion,
I'm pulled off balance by the propulsion.

HYPOKEIMENON THE BULL

We call him stock but when it's him and me
on an open field he is master of the moment –
fifteen metres I must carefully, without hastiness,
back up to thirty, so that from the fence
I can watch him in his shady kingdom
watching me. In my pique I imagine him
thinking: seen off another of you ridiculous
two-legs perched on that trundling
piece of metal with the buzzing noise
                    that hurts my ears so!

But is that really what stock think?
And would he even remember having seen
a two-leg before? He may reign in that grove
for the remainder of my shift
                but if bovine memory
hadn't been so reliably non-existent
would his roasting flesh have fed and consecrated
                the human empire for millennia?
        I offer thee his testicles, Mighty Helios!

I'm being precious (and besides no one saw).
The sentience of a being uncluttered by memory
is a direct line to first principles,
                and his principle is a simple one –
to *mass*. Even the seed he's seasonally compelled
to shoot serves to propagate another generation

of massives. For in the bull matter finds
the proudest incarnation of its most intrinsic
property, inertia. So if he crash the fence
and his status in the imperial ledgers slip
from stock to feral he'll be the universe itself
        eyeballing in the shooter's crosshairs.

SNAKE!

What a presence!
   Never could I not see it
       the black gleam of it –
one of the sun's freakiest machines –
  a thousand tendons
pistoning a long-linked bone-chain
    a snap of vivid flesh
           for a glove –
  muscular mass-whips
heat-spiked across the lawn
        quick as a grass fire –
Death if I got in its way.

For it's the surprise
  of this peaceful orchard.
My heart would stop
at the thought of a punctured ankle
even before the venom
       seized it –
  a Big-Bang Plasma Bomb.

  How picturesquely
these trees would shade my corpse.

READING *THE GITAGOVINDA* IN KUNUNURRA

The lamplight captures us –
you sleep, I read –
Krishna kisses the beads on Radha's breasts.

Cool atmospheres usher in the night –
scented with eucalyptus and hibiscus flower
the agonies, rage and pleasures
                of elsewhere streets.

Elsewhere streets beckon me –
agonies, rage and pleasures
disperse to other streets –
I run onto porches
             through open doors
flop onto mattresses with other men's wives
kiss cow-eyed girls under streetlights
flee their brawling boyfriends –
night's passions scented with eucalyptus
               and hibiscus flower

Kamadhenu's envoys be in the mulga
                 where I hide –
they are the earth's silent cows –
pale forms loom in Miriwoong moon.

The moon is uncanny in passing hours –

'I knew you'd return.
    I have dressed for you;
        I wear an anklet and a wedding ring.'

Krishna strokes Radha's navel and hair.
The lamp is off –
        the dark bed captures them.

SHORTCUT THROUGH MIRIMA CEMETERY

Should I think at the dead our transit
means no disrespect; or should I speak it aloud
just to be sure? My daughter walks her bike
past their graves innocent of greed or blasphemy
or any ill feeling in her heart. If she stops
to take the plastic flowers the wind has scattered
and tucks them into her basket, it's to adorn
a garden of dolls drinking tea and riding trains
                on our loungeroom floor.

So is it fair to speak for us, when I'm really
only speaking for me? Is that why I won't look
at the visitor seated on a bench? Though the sun
plays tricks under those trees, my skin pucks
at what my mind dares to think; to apologise
for a presumed transgression imputes suspicion
and jealousy to the dead, signifying the impurity
of my own heart, an aperture of bad faith
through which fate's emulsions can stain my sight.
I'll whisper a prayer for myself instead
                and hurry us along.

AIR MINUS TIME

The fans seem oblivious of seconds –
they whirr as if a second is a second,
each oscillation consigns another one
to the past. But really, time is as sluggish
as my head on a damp pillow, infuriating
as a droplet of sweat running into
my underwear elastic. These things
are the true measurements of what the day
flows in; heat bands that wend through
all spaces, rubbing my skin and reddening
my eyes, separate time from air,
render all digits and units irrelevant
and leave me engulfed in a static unframed
here-now visualising my body
as a combusting test dummy. So fans,
continue spinning in that dimension
of rationed segments; I'll find you
translated from the meter to our next bill;
but while I can see you turn
you have no impact on any other sense.

THE REMOTE ACCOUNTANT'S HUSBAND

I'm a househusband in the Kimberley;
I descend to my meditative washing line.
While the stomps of mother–daughter strife
thump the floorboards above my head
I am at peace, shirtless and perspiring,
pegging the underwear and shorts,
my nose wrinkling at the resins and rot
of the tropics, my ear tuning in
to the one-note cicada choir; I can ignore
the shouting, even not concern myself
with that concerning crash,
for it is enough for me to breathe and do
one thing at a time in this thundering sauna –
one peg – one fold – repeat –
as all senses become one surface
for rashes to prickle and sweat drops to trickle.

THE SLUT'S DREAM

If I wish really hard maybe I can steer us
through the day from my bed; think the kids up,
breakfasted, dressed and off to school,
my wife to work; and all day, as the heat cloys
through every pore of space
between the walls, the blinds and the door
I'll never open, administer from an adjacent room
inverse to the volume of the house. I can dream
the manky sheets unravelling along the mattresses
until they're smooth, the dishes marching
through the hot suds to dry on the rack,
vegetables chopping themselves
for tonight's casserole and toys climbing back
into their baskets for the next deployment;
outside, bluebirds lift the washing
in their tender beaks to meet the pegs on the line.
If I should wake to see the doorhandle turning
know it's the broom and pan entering
                    to sweep up the wool.

READING *TO THE LIGHTHOUSE*
ON CASUARINA FORESHORE, DARWIN

She'll kill them all!
She'll flip the boat,
and waves, waves, thumping waves
will close over every remaining
                Ramsey head!

She wants to be where we are now;
far above on a hill
so distance renders liquid corrugations
a smooth pane of blue
and human adventure
a speck in God's indifferent eye.
She places the painter here instead
as a gift for representing her best self,
while she, the writer, stays close
to the wrangling in the rigging,
the unsteady rump shifts at the gybe,
and there thinks her worst thoughts.
        The beast at the helm,
he's the one she wants. Except
he's surrounded himself with the kids.

Now I, the reader, am a god too –
getting out of that boat
is easy; I slip in a bookmark
        and gaze on another smooth sea,

one no one sails or swims in
and so remains forever background.
                    But if I'm also
a patriarch on a family holiday
and maybe I've tyrannised
with my petulance, mood swings
and toddler egoism, where
would the goddess who writes me
avenge my impiety?
              On the long roads perhaps?
              A momentary blink
at a wraith,
the drowned day-dress and hair,
                    on the edge of vision?

I return to the boat
with the playthings of Mrs Woolf's
moral universe and find she still
hasn't decided what to do to them.
Those non-human cities of coral,
barely a metre beneath James Ramsey's
          coursing fingers,
                    look so cosmopolitan.

THE INTERNATIONAL YEAR OF GLASS
Composed for the Kununurra Agricultural Show, 2022

You block the wind
But not the light

Correct the flaws
In human sight

You bring to view
The very small

Reduce a planet
To the size of a ball.

That's how us moderns
Think of you

As many forms
Of seeing through.

But Artisans
Of ancient civics

Saw mysticism
In your puzzling physics

By nature scattered
In water and sand

The strangest stone
Held by human hand

Seemed only two thirds
Actually there

Weight and hardness
But otherwise air.

Fashioned with fire
They praised their deity

In bead and vessel
Of transparent beauty.

TRIBUTE

My pen will pause at the end of this line,
the fan will complete another turn –
but where will I be
when the pen seeks the line below
and the blades slice the air once more?

I call on you, triple-twined river,
            to answer that;
you flow both for your archaic self,
and for wild and cultivated things to grow –
now aid me be what I'm meant to be,
by being your third being, *force* –
pound your atomic self through turbines
            to illuminate and cool,
then my thralling words can flow
            to the last line of the page.

HALF A PLANET AWAY

I

How will we withstand a remote town's
contraction? It's hard to point to the way
we're dismissed, locals don't exactly
turn their backs in Coles; it's a tangible sense
of introversion, a closing off into mateship
groups, a phenomenon not always apparent,
hidden by the vegan calendar
and secondee gatherings at groovy
Tarantino screenings, but now the only social
pattern in town – the school with its pathways
to existing rural industries (or boarding school
for the squires' kids). It's like the clockwork
country folk had their keys wound again
to continue the suspended akubra doff,
the excluding mate-talk between butcher,
baker, hairdresser and postmistress,
smiling recognition glancing our cheeks
to the worthies behind our shoulders,
while we remain stranded between redundancy
and exile, half a planet away from fellowship.

II

Imagine their houses look like night teeth
sticking crooked and top heavy
each with one trapezium window light
and they the hiding folk who switch off
the lights when skelectro branches
fingering the mountain's crown show
a host of ghouls on their galloping steeds
scythes aloft make merry in the strobing night.
To church! To pub! To the one true-blue Muster!
Heed not the cheating words of out-of-towners
and pray away the daughter's gay
           half a planet away from reason!

KUNUNURRA SKIES

The way the cloud bunches up
behind the bluff makes me realise
we're so far away
we might as well be miniatures;
squeaky-voiced Lilliputians
in exquisitely rendered
mini-clothes, tapping the pointy
ends of eggs and putting about
in dinky cars on streets
of a matchstick town a man
in rubber reptile suit is going
to stomp and kick to pieces.
The cloud augments cloud
in fluffy cloud fashion, intimate
as cream smoke from
a magician's hat, propagating itself
out of absolutely nothing.

It won't rain. It never rains
(until it does), but that's another life
on a scale for towns in outer space.

OLD HANDS

Old hands resting on seated haunches
or fidgeting for tobacco and paper
they haven't rolled in fifteen years,
know that until the water table recedes
and muddy tracks harden there's little
for them to do; the grass stays unmowed
and trees remain unlopped, machines
sit in sheds and fertiliser stays in bags.
So it's tea after tea in the warming shed
and hours flourished by the radio news;
they can tamp the young hand's zeal
and otherwise appear busy enough,
but it's tricky hoping for the whiling day
as the Department continues its grudging pay,
for no one, *no one*, God forbid,
                will dare wish the rain away.

THE QUEEN RAIN

The rain is our Queen –
she wears the sky like a great grey coat
leans over the sunlit trees
and pokes their tops with electric sticks.

Relieved against the thundering seconds
the subjects await the water monarch –
cicadas still sing
    wallabies still watch
          cow tails idly flick at flies –

For her reign is the drenching
her state the monsoon
and she rambles through her realm
              in big wet galoshes.

WATER PLANET

It must've been a big drop
blobbing through space
for when it splashed on our rock
it became our rivers, lakes and seas.

For aeons it has tried to escape
climbing through the heat
in a bid to resume its celestial course
and become its own globby planet.

Behold its absconding vapours
change into drenching doona skies –
watch it spit electricity in a rage
and thrash our rock with its rain;

for its terrestrial exile abides
(as mass is insensitive to Right),
and wherever its sloshing restlessness wet
libidinous things endlessly beget.

KIMBERLEY CURRICULUM

1. Logistics and Myth

We are the faraway
where the freight trucks come to stay –
distance from Perth
makes the freight trucks mythical.

5am. In the thin dawn
the nearing doors
the grinding gears
the reversing bleeps
declare the heads of broccoli
and tins of baby corn spears
here to fill the slots –
the store hand flicks away her fag
and moves to pull the bolts.

In another time
another country
a freight truck faraway
grumbles along the mythical highway.

2. The Graduate's Care

Facebook requests
for tarps and lifts
show nothing of the political

except the perennial complaint
of trespass – a quick scroll
of propertied grievance
ends with an icon of a gun.

8.30am. Her new law degree
is the Right
against this Might,
but just this once,
against protocol,
she'll take the trouble
to adjust the mute boy's collar.

Inside the court
the boy's peers are gathering,
        texting managers.

3. AGM Near the Tanami Desert

The air-con drips.
        The board prays.
The screensaver fish blow bubbles.
Next on the agenda –
who wrote the poison pen letter,
and whose 34-year-old son
threw rocks
on the Reverend's roof.
It's 10am before the accountant
breaks it to them:
they're trading while insolvent.

A resident, 73, thinks –
The Tanami, he's my brother;

I see him, out the open door,
big man in the saddle,
leading dust from the herd.
Aunty's at the door
with towels and a jug of water.

4. A Farmhand at Ceres Farm

A pale moon at midday,
delicate as a soap bubble.
That's all the old blue sky reveals –
    the archaic saturation.

We must grow the crops
on our rock, tilt the water
running on its surface
in our direction
     for our elevation
and our prismatic concentration
out there to underscore us.

So muses the poet
as he shears the transect
of wheat. His employer's name
    tickles him –
could these cracks of earth
lead to the tiled halls
and cavernous bed
of Proserpina's captivity?

5. Workshop Fugue

The black grease furnace, 2pm.
The black grease cracks
in his fingers; fingers worrying,
working that fused cylinder
          under the manifold – there!

          Oh God, not again –
I've lived another life –
Like paint flaking off,
another paint job underneath.
I'm swimming somewhere.
Now. In a lake, with my sisters.

"You alright, Mick?"
Young guy under the bonnet –
Oh Christ, who? Connell's boy.

The shed takes shape again –
the big fan, the roller door chain,
the gold Patrol in the sun.
"Yeah. Cunt's cooked his engine."

6. Marking Late

Crocodiles. Boab trees.
Kangaroos. Blake Somers'
     is the best one –
a Gilbert's dragon's propeller legs.

Before her, tomorrow's
attentive portraits
and distracted profiles

are all at their vacant desks.
She chides her weakness
but the headache persists.

So her gaze lengthens
with the veranda shadows.
It's the surface
of Mercury out there –
        even in air-con
the peak heat
radiates off the glass.

Goodness, the cleaners.
        4.30 already.

7. Overtime – Parks and Wildlife

An old man spotted –
proprietorial hands on hips –
        right near the bank.
"He'll be tonight's dinner
if he doesn't stand back."
Splash! goes the calf's head
        in the black water,
                the whiz of straps
on the gunnel. Sinews
and shirts wet with sweat,
and that smell; unmistakable –
everyone can smell
the dinner they'd be –
    bone, blood and tripe
        dipped in river soup.

The spotlight on the water is a shaft
of algal sightlessness, and yet
                              the water watches.

8. Constable x

Locker-room advice: transfer
at the first dangerous thoughts.

Just lately she's begun to feel
            machined –
            an exhilaration so far
from the academy's thrown hats
and naïve joy of the pledge.

Power is a brooding engine
the pop of taut leather
the smell of her partner's sweat;
a thrill purer than any stone.
It's that simple, and that dangerous.

Radio codes distill
            unspeakable things.

Spotted in the headlights
faces of the enemy –
                  insolence and fear.

9. Logistics and Myth

The loneliest fluorescence
encones a midnight bowser

and a keypad
five years of northern sun
        has aged to twenty.

What mortal thought
is worthy of living a myth?
What's a consignment form,
or an eftpos transaction,
    but ontic spots
on the planet's longest shadow.
He exists the moment
the funds are authorised,
then the black up ahead
    erases his truck and haul.

They grind back into being
in a far town's granite dawn.

THE BIGGEST WORLD UNDER A FAN

My thoughts drift wordlessly.
It's so hard to get a hold
on dozy images I consider
resorting to 'write not writing',
or 'having nothing to begin with',
just to get something on the page.

Come forth, leading image, before
my heavy head drop on the table,
and my heavy body settle, so bone
and flesh massive in the last unnatural
position I can't muster the energy
                    to heave from.

There, that's it! Now capture it
in a quick phrase – the spiky
twelve-tone pipings of pipit, plover
and friarbird in the spore haze
of the orchards, sourced from one
of a handful of thought experiments
during this morning's mowing.

I sat on the idle mower and listened.
My phone stayed in my pocket.
A dimension that bore no relationship
to the time on its display
foregrounded itself to my senses.

The hush, spangled with bird calls,
                    resumed.

My mind sought universals –
that human things carry on besides,
within, but never, God forbid,
                    determine nature;
that while cultivation is human,
growth and death are not;
all the grafting, mulching, watering,
the chemical enhancements,
can only nudge natural things
towards productive growth,
while nature's minions
such as termites and wallabies
destroy for the glory
of their dishevelled empress
who would, if she could, reign over us
as solitary and starving brutes.

My mind beheld the terror –
that if humans make
a counter-nature with their things,
seek and split and suck
all her myriad energies
into planet-smothering prostheses,
the call of natural reason
within humans must forestall
a war for dead rock and vacuum.

Then I looked beyond. I observed
how the paddocks shimmered
with the white moths,

and how the power poles
of the highway seemed to stitch
the plain to the pale ridges
        of another country.
I thought, there are many worlds
in the one world – some bigger
than the one that subsumes them;
they come to being in every perception,
and grow cosmic in particulars.

The birds embroidered the biggest world –
       the one my page captures –
with music of exquisite indifference.

I'm dozing now.
So, was that a tired old thing
to write, or something beautiful?

THE LAST STREETLIGHT AND THE INEXPRESSIBLE

Synecdoche of all that powers and secures us –
utopia of shoulder and road.

What's weird is the boundary
        of its magician-click booth,
how it illuminates here, veils out there,
but gives out there preternatural eyes.

It is the quick else that flows in air
but is irreducible to air –
 nor is it time, though time mingles
                in the squiggles of sticks and black.

What streams is discrete –
summoned from the substance of the river
        a luminous hum
where refugees from immensity come,
                the tinks of their bodies on globe.

ACKNOWLEDGEMENTS

First of all, I wish to thank my wife, Meredith. Not only has she provided crucial inspiration (and modelling) for the material in this volume, she has supported me without complaint for nearly two decades of near obscurity. I couldn't have achieved this publication without her.

Nor could I have achieved it without the tireless and cheerful support of Peter Jeffery OAM. Ever since we became friends at Murdoch University back in the early 1990s, Peter has been unwavering in his belief in me. I hope the publication of this volume is a small vindication of the time and energy he has devoted to my work.

I also wish to thank Georgia Richter from Fremantle Press, who saw potential in the small group of poems I submitted eighteen months ago. Her editing of the volume has been vigorous and illuminating.

Finally, thanks to the (mostly unpaid) personnel at WA Poets for running The Perth Poetry Club and the online journal *Creatrix* where many of these poems had their first outings.

The Traherne epigram is from *Christian Ethicks* by Thomas Traherne, edited by Carol L. Marks and Guffey, Cornell University Press, 1968. And the Yeats quote in the Author's Note is from W.B. Yeats, *Selected Poems*, ed. Timothy Webb, Penguin Books, 1961, p. 57.

All poems were composed in the Kununurra Public Library on the traditional lands of the Miriwoong nation. I offer this volume in honour of Miriwoong elders past and present.

First published 2024 by
FREMANTLE PRESS

Fremantle Press Inc. trading as Fremantle Press
PO Box 158, North Fremantle, Western Australia, 6159
fremantlepress.com.au

Cover art 'Beyond Small' by Priya Wilson
Designed by Karmen Lee, Karma Design, hellokarma.com

A catalogue record for this
book is available from the
NATIONAL National Library of Australia
LIBRARY
OF AUSTRALIA

ISBN 9781760992897 (paperback)
ISBN 9781760992903 (ebook)

GOVERNMENT OF
WESTERN AUSTRALIA

lotterywest

Fremantle Press is supported by the Western Australian State
Government through the Department of Cultural Industries, Tourism
and Sport.

Fremantle Press respectfully acknowledges the Whadjuk people of the
Noongar nation as the Traditional Owners and Custodians of the land
where we work in Walyalup.

www.ingramcontent.com/pod-product-compliance
Lightning Source LLC
Chambersburg PA
CBHW021157090426
42740CB00008B/1126